THE
SOLAR
SYSTEM

Anna Claybourne

Evans

TITLES IN THE SCIENCE IN FOCUS SERIES:
DIGITAL TECHNOLOGY   THE EARTH'S RESOURCES   GENETICS
THE HUMAN BODY   THE SOLAR SYSTEM   WEATHER

Produced for Evans Brothers Limited by
Monkey Puzzle Media Limited
Gissing's Farm, Fressingfield
Suffolk IP21 5SH, UK

Published by Evans Brothers Limited
2A Portman Mansions
Chiltern Street
London W1U 6NR

First published 2006
© copyright Evans Brothers 2006

British Library Cataloguing in Publication Data
Claybourne, Anna
The solar system– (Science in focus)
1.Solar system– Juvenile literature
I.Title
523.2

ISBN 0 237 52726 X
13-digit ISBN (from 1 January 2007) 978 0 237 52726 6

Editor: Steve Parker
Designer: Jane Hawkins
Picture researcher: Lynda Lines
Artwork by Michael Posen

Picture acknowledgements:
Digital Vision front cover centre left and bottom left, 3, 13 left, 14 bottom, 15, 17 bottom, 20, 23, 31
top, 35 bottom, 37; Getty Images 14 top (Antonio M Rosario/The Image Bank), 17 top (Firstlight);
NASA front cover top left, 8, 9, 10, 11, 16, 19 top, 21 both, 22, 25, 27, 38, 39 bottom, 40;
Photolibrary.com 13 right (Walter Bibikow); Science Photo Library front cover main image (David A
Hardy), 6 (David A Hardy), 7 top (Science, Industry and Business Library/New York Public Library), 12
(Mark Garlick), 26 (Detlev Van Ravenswaay), 28 (Roger Harris), 29 (Detlev Van Ravenswaay), 32
(Robin Scagell), 33 (Detlev Van Ravenswaay), 34, 36 (David A Hardy), 39 top (Julian Baum), 41
(NASA); Still Pictures 7 bottom (Astrofoto), 18 (Astrofoto), 19 bottom (Astrofoto), 31 bottom (H R
Bramaz).

CONTENTS

SUN AT THE CENTRE

The Solar System is the part of space that contains our planet, the Earth. It is made up of a star called the Sun, and all the space objects that circle around it.

STICKING TOGETHER

The Solar System is centred on the Sun which lights up our world every day. The system includes nine planets that go around, or orbit, the Sun. It also includes many smaller orbiting objects such as moons, rocks, and bits of ice and dust. These many different parts of the Solar System are always on the move, yet they do not fly apart. They are kept together in one big cluster by a pulling force which every object has, called gravity. The Sun is so big, it has massive gravity. It keeps all of the planets and other parts of the Solar System moving around it, following their regular pathways or orbits through space.

▼ The Solar System is shaped like a flat disk with the Sun shining in the middle. From nearest the Sun to farthest, the planets are Mercury (1), Venus (2), Earth (3), Mars (4), Jupiter (5), Saturn (6), Uranus (7), Neptune (8) and Pluto (9).

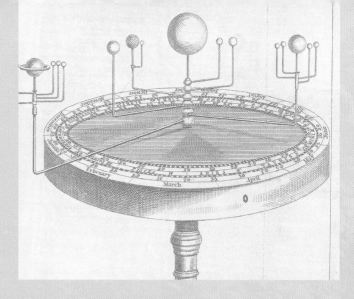

▶ An orrery is a mechanical model of the Solar System. This 1720s version has only six planets plus their moons. At the time it was made, the three outermost planets had not been discovered.

SUN AND PLANETS

The Sun is a star, just like the stars we see twinkling as tiny points of light on a cloudless night. But the Sun is so near to the Earth that it looks like a giant ball of flame in the daytime sky. The nearest planets to the Earth are Mercury, Mars and Venus. All parts of the Solar System have been studied with telescopes, and all the planets except one have been visited by space probes (small spacecraft without people). Scientists have been able to find out much about these planets.

EVIDENCE FOCUS

SOLAR SYSTEM MODEL

In pictures and models of the Solar System, like the one opposite, the Sun and planets are usually shown close together. But in real life, they are very far apart. Imagine a soccer ball is the Sun. Measure a distance of 24 metres from it, and hold up a peppercorn or similar sized object. On a tiny scale, these are the sizes and positions of the Sun and Earth.

HOW BIG IS THE SOLAR SYSTEM?

Compared to distances on Earth, the Solar System is very, very big! It measures more than 13,000 million kilometres across. If a person could walk across it from one side to the other, without stopping, it would take more than a third of a million years.

However, compared to the whole of space, the Solar System is tiny. It is a very small part of a galaxy (a huge whirling cloud of stars) called the Milky Way. And the Milky Way itself is just one of millions and millions of galaxies across the incredible vastness of space.

▼ The Milky Way galaxy is a giant spiral of billions of stars and other objects, whirling around in space. Our Solar System is about halfway between its centre and its edge.

THE
UNIVERSE

The Universe is all of space and everything in it. In other words, the Universe is everything that exists. It is made up of all the galaxies, stars, planets and other objects in all of space – everything and everywhere.

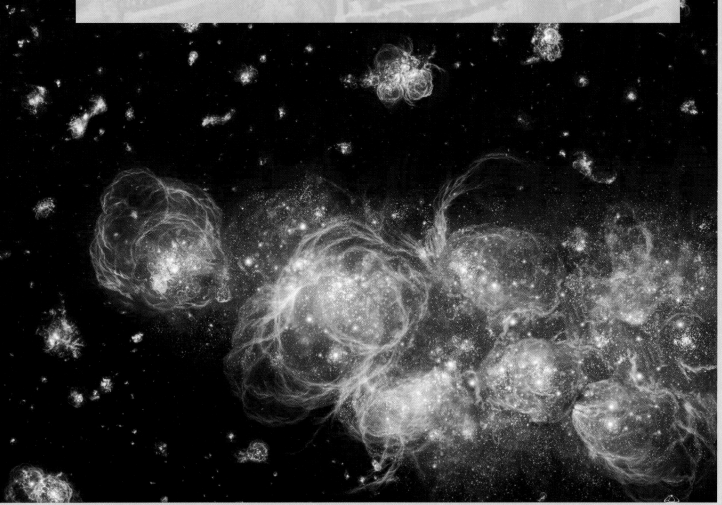

▲ This imaginary scene shows what the Universe might have looked like, just after the Big Bang. Of course, it was so long ago, no one can be sure!

THE BIG BANG

Scientists think that the Universe has not always existed. According to their main idea, or theory, the Universe and everything in it formed in a huge, sudden explosion called the 'Big Bang'. This happened around 13,000 million years ago. Time also started with the Big Bang. This means before the Big Bang, space and time did not exist.

Just after the Big Bang, the Universe was a huge, dense fireball. Gradually it started to cool and spread out. The wispy clouds of matter began to form separate objects such as stars. These parts of the Universe are still getting farther apart, which suggests that today, the Universe is still growing.

▲ Nebulae are clouds of gases, dust and other tiny particles. This photo shows a 'butterfly' nebula which may have formed as one star smashed into another.

OBJECTS IN THE UNIVERSE

The Universe contains several different kinds of objects, such as galaxies, stars, planets and nebulae. A galaxy is a name for a vast cluster of stars. There are many millions of galaxies in the Universe. A star is a giant ball of burning gas. A planet is a large space object that goes around a star. A nebula is a massive cloud of dust and gases floating in space.

Scientists believe that, as well as these objects, there must be more objects or substances in the Universe. However we have not been able to see or detect them yet. This mysterious, unseen material is called 'dark matter'.

UNIVERSE MYSTERIES

Many questions about the Universe wait to be answered. No one really knows how big it is or what shape it has. The farthest that our telescopes can see is almost 13,000 million light years away. The light year is a common measure of distance in space. One light year is the distance that light travels in one year. It is about 9,465 billion kilometres (that is, 9,465,000,000,000 kilometres).

Even if the Big Bang idea is correct, no one knows why it happened. Also, scientists are not sure about what will happen to the Universe in the future. Will it keep on growing, or stay the same size, or even start to shrink?

FACT FOCUS

BLACK HOLES

A black hole is a mysterious space object that forms when a star or group of stars collapses. After burning and shining brightly, the star shrinks or implodes, getting smaller and smaller. Its tremendous amount of matter (material) is squashed into such a small space that it has an incredible pulling force of gravity. This sucks in everything around it – even light. There are no black holes in the Solar System. The nearest one is about 1,600 light years away.

STARS AND PLANETS

The Universe contains billions and billions of stars and planets – far too many to see or count. And they do not last for ever. New ones are constantly forming, as old ones fade and die.

STARS

A star is like a giant ball of burning gas. It begins as a vast cloud-like nebula of dust and wispy, spread-out gases. As the dust and gases swirl around, some of them clump together under the force of gravity, and begin to form a ball. This gets hotter and starts to burn, like an explosion that carries on and on, giving out light and heat. The hottest stars burn white or blue-white. Slightly cooler stars burn yellow, orange or red. There are also different sizes of stars. Our Sun is small-to-medium. Stars bigger than the Sun are called giant or supergiant stars. Smaller ones are called dwarf stars.

▼ The Pistol Star near the centre of the Milky Way galaxy is far bigger than the Sun and shines 10 million times more brightly. But it is so far away from Earth, it can only be seen with a powerful telescope.

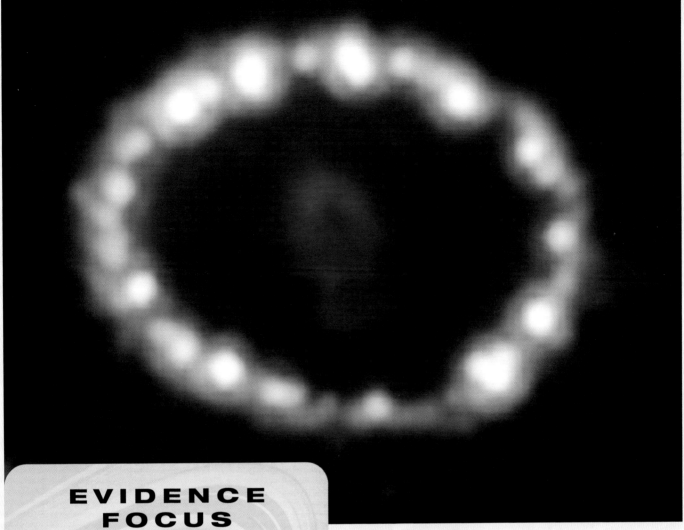

LIFE AND DEATH
Stars cannot live for ever. Big stars burn out quite fast, while small ones shine for longer. The Sun's total burning time is about 10,000 million years. At present, it is about halfway through its life. How stars die depends on their size. Small and medium-sized stars such as the Sun grow larger and redder. Their outer layers fly off into space. Finally all that is left is a small star called a white dwarf, which gradually fades away.

▲ A supernova is the death of a giant star in a tremendous explosion. We see it as a star that burns brighter for a time, maybe forming a cloud or a ring of clouds (as in this photograph).

Giant and supergiant stars turn into even more enormous red supergiants – then explode. The explosion is a brilliant flash in space called a supernova. After this, what is left of the star may form a very small but incredibly heavy object called a neutron star. Or the remains may shrink so tiny that they become a black hole (see page 9).

PLANETS
Planets are large objects that go around, or orbit, a star. Unlike stars, they do not burn. The planets of the Solar System probably formed from bits of dust, rock and gases left over after the Sun itself began. These materials circled the Sun, held in place by its gravity. Gradually the tiny pieces bumped into each other and formed fewer larger clumps, which slowly became the separate planets.

THE SUN

The Sun is the star in the middle of the Solar System. It is bigger than all the other objects in the Solar System added together, and its immense pull of gravity holds the Solar System together.

SUN FACTS

The Sun measures about 1.4 million kilometres across, which is about 109 times wider than Earth. More than a million Earths could fit inside the Sun. In the middle of the Sun the temperature is around 15 million degrees Celsius. Even the surface is about 5,500 degrees Celsius, which would instantly vapourise almost anything on Earth. Some areas of the Sun's surface are slightly cooler and appear as darker patches which grow and fade, called sunspots.

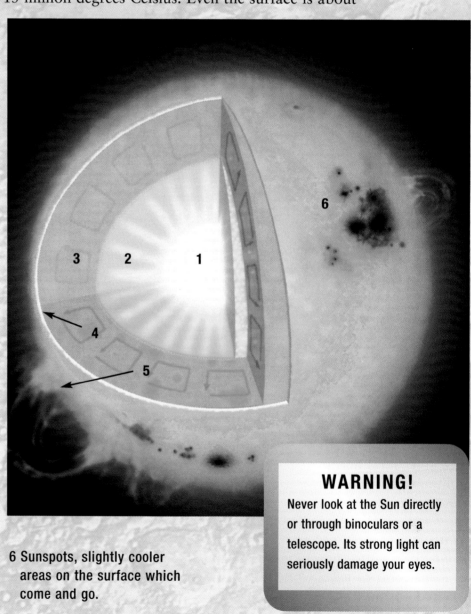

▶ Layers of the Sun, from centre outwards.

1 Core, where nuclear reactions produce energy.

2 Radiative zone, where energy rises and falls as it gradually radiates (spreads) outwards.

3 Convective zone, which carries or conveys energy to the Sun's surface.

4 Photosphere (meaning 'ball of light'), the visible shining surface of the Sun.

5 Corona, a faint glowing layer of gases surrounding the Sun.

6 Sunspots, slightly cooler areas on the surface which come and go.

WARNING!

Never look at the Sun directly or through binoculars or a telescope. Its strong light can seriously damage your eyes.

WHAT IS THE SUN MADE OF?

The Sun formed about 4,600 million years ago from a cloud of space dust and gases. Today it is mostly made up of two very light gases. Hydrogen forms almost three quarters of the Sun, and helium one quarter. Around one fiftieth of the Sun is made of other materials, such as iron.

▲ The Sun's energy takes about eight minutes to pass through space and reach the Earth. We feel its warmth and use its light to see by. Plants use its light energy to make their food by the process called photosynthesis.

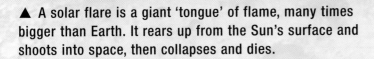

▲ A solar flare is a giant 'tongue' of flame, many times bigger than Earth. It rears up from the Sun's surface and shoots into space, then collapses and dies.

HEAT AND LIGHT

In the Sun's centre or core, atoms (tiny particles) of hydrogen smash together and join to make slightly larger atoms of helium. This process, called nuclear fusion, gives off huge amounts of energy. It escapes from the Sun mainly as heat and light. These are so powerful that we can see and feel them here on Earth – even though the Sun is 150 million kilometres away.

PULLING POWER

The more substance or mass an object has, the greater its pulling power or gravity. Because the Sun is so huge, its gravity is immense. It pulls on everything around it, within about 50,000 million kilometres. This pulling power holds onto the planets and the other objects in the Solar System, so they do not fly away into deep space.

INNER PLANETS

The inner planets are the four planets closest to the Sun – Mercury, Venus, Earth and Mars. They are among the smaller planets in the Solar System and because they are near the Sun, they are mostly quite warm.

MERCURY

Mercury is the nearest planet to the Sun, and moves around it fastest – once every 88 days. Its surface is blasted by the Sun's heat and is very dry. Its temperature ranges from minus 180 degrees Celsius at night, to over 450 degrees Celsius by day – which is more than seven times hotter than anywhere on Earth.

VENUS

Venus is the nearest planet to Earth, and about the same size as Earth. It has a rocky, desert-like surface, but we cannot see this through telescopes because of Venus's thick, heavy atmosphere (covering of gases). Venus also spins in the opposite direction to Earth and the other planets.

▲ Mercury's hot rocky surface is covered with bowl-shaped craters where space rocks have smashed into it.

◀ Venus is cloaked in an atmosphere of thick, orange, poisonous gases. These swirl around in never-ending patterns, far thicker than the clouds here on Earth.

EARTH

Our home planet is the only one in the Solar System, as far as we know, where life exists. Its atmosphere contains oxygen and carbon dioxide gases. The surface is made of a rocky layer or crust, floating on molten (melted) rocks below. Most of the crust is covered with water (see page 16).

▲ Mars has a red surface because its rocks and dust contain lots of the chemical iron oxide. On Earth, we call this rust.

MARS

Mars is smaller and colder than Earth. It is known as the Red Planet because of its red-brown colour. Its landscape is covered with dusty plains, hills, tall mountains and deep canyons. Mars has two tiny, lumpy moons called Deimos and Phobos.

FACT FOCUS

YEARS AND DAYS

The time it takes a planet to go around the Sun once is the length of a year on that planet. Our own Earth year is just over 365 days. A Mars year lasts 687 Earth days. Also, each planet spins or rotates around a line through its centre, called its axis. The time for one rotation is the length of a day on that planet. Venus spins so slowly that one Venus day lasts 243 Earth days.

PLANET FACTS

MERCURY

Diameter	4,880km
Distance from Sun	58 million km
Year length	88 Earth days
Day length	59 Earth days
Average surface temperature	167°C
Number of moons	0

VENUS

Diameter	12,104km
Distance from Sun	108 million km
Year length	225 Earth days
Day length	243 Earth days
Average surface temperature	464°C
Number of moons	0

EARTH

Diameter	12,756km
Distance from Sun	150 million km
Year length	1 Earth year (365.25 Earth days)
Day length	1 Earth day (24 hours)
Average surface temperature	15°C
Number of moons	1

MARS

Diameter	6,794km
Distance from Sun	228 million km
Year length	687 Earth days
Day length	1.03 Earth days
Average surface temperature	minus 63°C
Number of moons	2

THE EARTH AND THE MOON

As we learn more about other planets, we realise that Earth is very unusual. It has mild temperatures rather than extreme ones. It has water as a liquid rather than frozen as ice or boiled into steam. And it has living things.

HOW EARTH BEGAN

Earth probably formed at about the same time as the other Solar System planets and the Sun, around 4,600 million years ago. It began as a cloud of gases and dust which clumped together as it circled around the Sun. At first, Earth was mostly hot, glowing gases. Over time, it cooled and shrank.

Today, Earth has several layers inside. From the middle outwards these are an inner core of almost solid iron, an outer core of part-liquid iron, a layer of partly melted rock called the mantle, a very thin layer of solid rock known as the crust (which we live on), and various gases making up the atmosphere – the air around us.

◀ Earth's atmosphere is made of nitrogen, oxygen, carbon dioxide and other gases. Billions of water droplets float in it and clump together to form clouds which are seen from space as white swirls. This view of Earth shows the continents (main land masses) of North and South America.

CONSTANT CHANGE

The Sun's energy heats up Earth's air and water and makes them move around the planet as wind, clouds, rain, rivers, glaciers and ocean currents. Earth's surface is made of about a dozen massive curved pieces like huge jigsaw-shaped slabs of rock, called tectonic plates. These slowly move, push and grind against each other. Where they meet, their movements can cause earthquakes and volcanoes, or bend and buckle the rocks upward into new mountains.

▲ Earth's surface is always slowly moving. As rocks push together they bend up into giant mountains like the Himalayas, seen here from space.

THE MOON

A moon is an object that goes around a planet. Earth's moon is called the Moon, with a capital 'M'. It probably formed over 4,000 million years ago when the young Earth bumped into another planet-like object. Rocks and dust were flung into space and clumped together into the Moon, which Earth's gravity kept nearby. The Moon is a ball of cold, grey rock with no atmosphere. It is covered in craters where it has been hit over millions of year by rocks from space.

▶ The Moon orbits the Earth once every 28 days. In the same time, it spins around once. This means the same side of the Moon always points toward or faces the Earth.

EVIDENCE FOCUS

PHASES OF THE MOON

If you look at the Moon every night for 28 days, you will see that it appears to change shape, from a thin curved crescent or New Moon, to a round disc or Full Moon, and back again to an Old Moon. This happens because, as the Moon orbits Earth, sunlight falls on different parts of it. We can only see the sunlit parts – the rest is too dark.

MOON FACTS

Diameter	3,476km
Distance from Earth	384,400km
Time for one orbit	28 Earth days
Time for one rotation	28 Earth days
Average surface temperature	minus 20ºC

MERCURY TO MARS

The inner planets, Mercury, Venus and Mars, are the closest to us. So they are the planets which we have been able to study the most, and we are still uncovering their fascinating secrets.

MYSTERIOUS MERCURY

Mercury has been difficult to study properly, because it is so close to the Sun. The Sun's blinding light makes the planet hard to see, and can damage delicate telescopes. But in 1974–75 the space probe Mariner 10 flew past Mercury for a closer look. This was the first time people saw details of Mercury's surface. Mariner 10 found that Mercury had very little atmosphere and no water. The planet is made mainly of iron.

VEILED VENUS

The surface of Venus is hidden by the planet's thick, hazy atmosphere. This is full of clouds of dust, acids and gases from the planet's many active volcanoes. To find out more about Venus, space probes have scanned it using radar – radio signals bounced off the planet's surface and detected as 'echoes'. This has allowed us to map the craters, plains, volcanoes and mountain ranges beneath the thick clouds.

The space probe Magellan visited Venus in 1990–94. It saw that some volcanoes have unusual ridges around them, unlike anything on other planets. They are called arachnoid volcanoes, meaning spider-shaped, because the central volcano with its surrounding ridges looks like a giant spider.

◄ The inner planets are sometimes seen at dawn, shining like stars. They do not make their own light, but reflect the Sun's light. This photograph shows Mercury just above the treetops, and Venus next to the Moon which is at the top right.

▲ This Magellan radar picture shows two huge volcanoes on Venus. Sif Mons (left) is 300km across, and Gula Mons (right) is 3,000m high.

MARS QUESTIONS

Venus is the closest planet to Earth, but Mars is the one we know most about. In 1783, astronomer William Herschel suggested that dark areas he saw on Mars could be water, and that life might exist there. In 1877 another astronomer, Giovanni Schiaparelli, saw *canali* (Italian for 'channels') on Mars. Many people thought he meant 'canals' - and were convinced they had been built by aliens. From the 1970s, several space probes have explored the Martian surface. They found no liquid water or life. But they did show that, millions of years ago, Mars had liquid water.

◀ This giant 'scratch' on Mars, Valles Marineris, is a massive steep-sided canyon 4,000km long. It was probably formed as huge crusts of rocks on Mars pulled apart, just as rift valleys form on Earth.

THE GAS GIANTS

The 'gas giants' are four huge planets in the outer part of the Solar System. They get their name because they are mostly made of gases, rather than liquids or solids – and because they are so big.

This picture (not to scale) shows the gas giants much closer together than they really are. From upper right to lower left they are Jupiter with its colourful stripes, Saturn with its amazing rings, Uranus and Neptune.

JUPITER

Jupiter is the biggest planet in the Solar System. It could hold more than 1,300 Earths inside it. Like the other gas giants, its outer layers are made of gases, with a small rocky core at the centre. Jupiter's powerful gravity has pulled many passing objects towards it. Many have become the planet's moons.

SATURN

The second-largest planet in the Solar System, Saturn, is famous for its beautifully bright rings. These are made of millions of bits of ice and rock whirling around the planet. Saturn spins around so fast that it bulges out around its middle, or equator. This gives it an oval shape when it is viewed from the side.

◀ Jupiter's moon Ganymede, 5,260km across, is the largest moon in the whole Solar System. In fact it is bigger than some of the planets.

FACT FOCUS

MOONS OF THE GAS GIANTS

All the gas giants have lots of moons. This is partly because their large size means they have strong gravity, and pull a lot of objects towards them. Some of the moons are massive, like Ganymede, shown above. Astronomers regularly discover new moons around the gas giants.

▶ In July 2005 the Cassini probe photographed Enceladus, one of Saturn's smallest and closest moons. Just 500km across, the surface of this glistening frost-covered ball has craters, plains, long 'tiger stripe' cracks and piles of house-sized ice blocks.

URANUS

Icy-cold Uranus is not as big as Jupiter and Saturn, yet it is still four times wider than Earth. It is bright blue-green and has a hazy, smooth-looking surface. Unlike the other planets, which mostly spin upright, Uranus spins on its side, at right-angles to the Sun. Its 11 rings are much fainter than Saturn's, and were discovered in 1977.

NEPTUNE

Neptune, the smallest of the gas giants, can only be seen from Earth using a telescope or powerful binoculars. Like Uranus, it is extremely cold. Its intensely blue surface looks hazy and appears to be flat and calm.

PLANET FACTS

JUPITER

Diameter	143,000km
Distance from Sun	778 million km
Year length	11.9 Earth years
Day length	10 Earth hours
Average surface temperature	minus 110ºC
Number of moons	At least 63

SATURN

Diameter	120,500km
Distance from Sun	1,433 million km
Year length	29 Earth years
Day length	10 Earth hours
Average surface temperature	minus 140ºC
Number of moons	At least 47

URANUS

Diameter	51,100km
Distance from Sun	2,900 million km
Year length	84 Earth years
Day length	17 Earth hours
Average surface temperature	minus 200ºC
Number of moons	At least 27

NEPTUNE

Diameter	49,500km
Distance from Sun	4,500 million km
Year length	165 Earth years
Day length	16 Earth hours
Average surface temperature	minus 200ºC
Number of moons	At least 13

BIGGEST OF THE GIANTS

At first glance Jupiter and Saturn, the two largest planets, look different. Yet in many ways they are quite alike, being similar in size and their mainly gaseous structure.

GREAT BALLS OF GAS

Like all the giant planets, Jupiter and Saturn are mostly gases – probably hydrogen and helium. An approaching space probe would simply sink down through the surface. But deep below the surface, the gases become more compressed (squashed), and are almost like liquids. In the middle of each of these planets is a small, solid core.

Heat from deep inside Jupiter and Saturn causes their outer layers of gas to swirl around as winds and storms. The fast spinning speed of these planets makes the storms separate into bands that look like streaks and stripes across the surface. In some areas, the clouds form large, whirling circles or oval shapes. The largest of these is on Jupiter and is called the Great Red Spot.

PLANETS WITH RINGS

Saturn is most famous for its rings. In fact all the gas giants have rings, but Saturn's are the brightest. Jupiter's three rings are very faint and are not visible from Earth. They were discovered in 1979 when the two Voyager space probes flew past. Jupiter's rings are probably made of dust knocked off its moons when they are hit by space rocks.

◀ Jupiter's Great Red Spot, which is to the upper left of this photograph, is three times bigger than Earth. Near it, mysterious white ovals come and go. One is shown here towards the lower right.

SATURN'S RINGS

Huge and bright, the rings of Saturn are easily seen from Earth with a telescope or even through binoculars. The big gap between the main rings is called the Cassini Division, and the smaller gap is the Encke Division. Each main ring is made up of thousands of smaller 'ringlets'. Space probes show that the rings probably formed when a passing comet got caught in Saturn's gravity millions of years ago, and broke into countless pieces.

▼ Chunks of ice and rock in Saturn's rings range from tiny specks to boulders as big as a bus. The whole disc of rings is nearly one million kilometres across, yet hardly one kilometre thick.

NOW YOU SEE THEM...

Like the Earth and most other planets, Saturn is tilted slightly to one side. As it moves around the Sun, we view it from the Earth at different angles. This means we see the underside of the rings, followed by the edges, then the upper sides, and so on. The rings look thinnest when they appear edge-on to us, about once every 15 years.

HISTORY FOCUS

THE 'EARS' OF SATURN

Great astronomer Galileo was the first to see Saturn's rings, when he studied the planet with an early telescope in 1610. However, he could not see them clearly and was puzzled. He decided they could be two moons, one on each side of the planet. He called them Saturn's 'ears'.

BLUE AND FAR AWAY

Uranus and Neptune are smaller and farther than Jupiter and Saturn, and much harder to see. They were only discovered after telescopes were invented – Uranus in 1781 and Neptune in 1846.

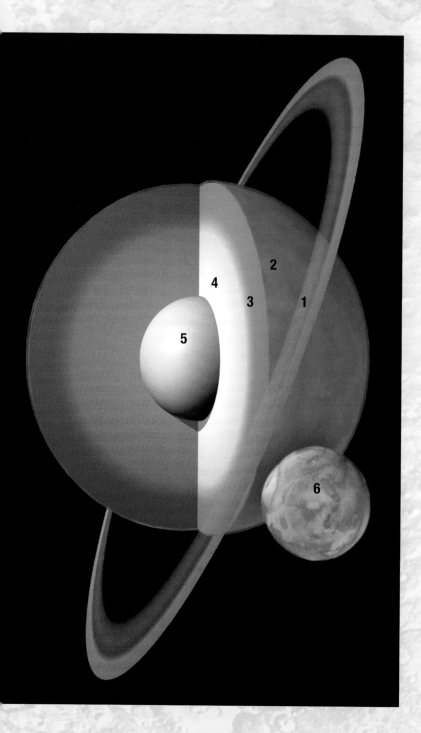

BLUE PLANETS

Unlike Jupiter and Saturn, which are orange or yellow, Uranus is bright blue-green and Neptune is deep blue. This is because, as well as hydrogen and helium gases, these planets also have crystals of the chemical methane in their atmosphere. But like the other gas giants, Uranus and Neptune have a rocky core deep inside.

RINGS AND MOONS

The rings of Uranus and Neptune are much smaller and fainter than those of Saturn. They are made of rocks and dust orbiting around the planets. Uranus and Neptune are also surrounded by numerous moons. So far Uranus is known to have over 27 moons, and Neptune more than 13. Most of these moons have a solid, rocky surface.

◀ This diagram shows the layers inside Uranus, which are very similar to those within its neighbour Neptune.

KEY
1 Faint rings – Uranus spins on its side and 'rolls around the Sun'.
2 Outer atmosphere of hydrogen and helium gases and methane crystals.
3 Gases squeezed almost into liquid.
4 Heavier layer of water frozen as ice and other semi-solid substances.
5 Solid core of rock.
6 Earth shown at same scale.

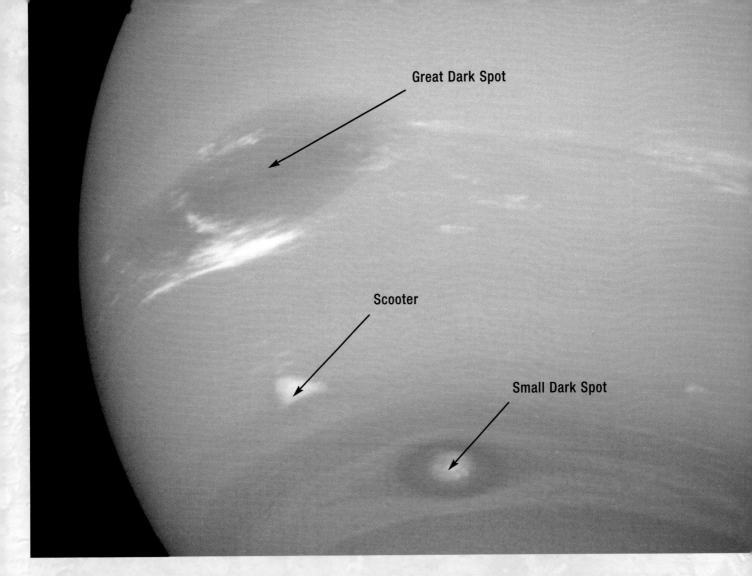

Great Dark Spot

Scooter

Small Dark Spot

▲ This photograph of Neptune shows the Great Dark Spot on the upper left, the Scooter below it, and the Small Dark Spot on the lower right.

SMOOTH OR STORMY?

At first glance, Uranus and Neptune look calm and less stormy than Jupiter and Saturn. But space probes such as Voyager 2, which flew past Neptune in 1989, found fast, swirling storms on the surface. Neptune, in particular, is incredibly windy. Heat from inside the planet stirs up its gases, creating wind speeds of up to 2,000 kilometres per hour – the fastest on any planet. Voyager 2 also found a white cloud nicknamed the Scooter, which zooms around Neptune every 16 hours.

ICY WORLDS

Although Uranus and Neptune have heat deep inside, they are very cold on the surface. They are so far away from the Sun that it barely warms them at all. On both planets the outer layer is around minus 200 degrees Celsius – over twice as cold as anywhere on Earth. Neptune's largest moon, Triton, is one of the coldest places in the Solar System, at minus 230 degrees Celsius.

FACT FOCUS

LONG ORBITS
Compared to Earth, the gas giants make long trips around the Sun. Although they hurtle through space at great speed – Jupiter travels at 47,000 kilometres per hour – they take many Earth years to complete one orbit. In fact Neptune has not had time to complete one full orbit since it was discovered by astronomer Johann Galle in 1846.

OUT ON THE EDGE

Beyond the four great gas giants, at the edge of the Solar System, are two much smaller space objects called Pluto and Sedna. Some scientists say they are planets – and others say they are not. The argument depends on how big a planet should be. One view is that an object below a certain size going around the Sun is not a true planet, but another type of space rock, such as an asteroid.

PLUTO

Pluto, discovered in 1930, is made mostly of rock and ice. It is smaller than any other main planet, and also smaller than many of the other planets' moons, including our own Moon. Yet Pluto has a large moon too, called Charon, which is about half as wide as itself. Besides its tiny size, Pluto is unusual because its orbit around the Sun is tilted at a different angle to the orbits of the other planets. Also, the orbit is much more elliptical or 'oval', so Pluto's distance from the Sun varies greatly. In fact, for a small part of its journey, Pluto goes

▲ Pluto's surface is made of frozen gases surrounding a layer of frozen water, with a large core of rock. Its largest moon, Charon, is the biggest moon in the Solar System compared to the planet it orbits.

inside Neptune's orbit. During this time, Pluto is not the farthest planet from the Sun.

THE KUIPER BELT

Out at the far edge of the Solar System, beyond the orbit of Neptune, lies the Kuiper Belt. This is believed to contain thousands of lumps of rock and ice, all orbiting the Sun.

▲ This imaginary picture shows what Sedna may look like. It could have a moon (upper centre). The Sun (upper right) looks like a slightly brighter version of an ordinary star.

SEDNA

In 2003 scientists discovered a new, very distant, planet-like object orbiting the Sun. It has a huge, oval-shaped orbit and is over twice as far from the Sun as Pluto. The new object was called 2003 VB12. Some scientists and newspapers claimed it was the Solar System's tenth planet. So in 2004 it was renamed Sedna. But most experts disagree with this. They say that Sedna is too small, too distant and too different to be a true planet.

FACT FOCUS

NAMES OF THE GODS

Apart from Earth, the planets have been named after gods worshipped by ancient peoples. For example, the fastest planet, Mercury, was named after the speedy messenger of the Roman gods. When object 2003 VB12 was named, experts chose Sedna. She is the goddess of the ocean for the Inuit people of Earth's far north, around the Arctic. This is very suitable since Sedna is so cold.

PLANET FACTS

PLUTO

Diameter	2,390km
Distance from Sun	4,436 to 7,375 million km
Year length	248 Earth years
Day length	6.4 Earth days
Average surface temperature	about minus 225ºC
Number of moons	3

SEDNA

Diameter	about 1,500km
Distance from Sun	11,500 million to 135,000 million km
Year length	10,500 Earth years
Day length	10 Earth hours
Average surface temperature	predicted as minus 240ºC
Number of moons	Unknown, probably 0 or 1

ASTEROIDS

Asteroids are lumps of rock or metal zooming through space around the Sun. They are the Solar System's 'leftovers' – bits of dust and gases that clumped together but did not end up forming planets or moons.

DISCOVERING ASTEROIDS

Astronomer Giuseppe Piazzi was the first to discover an asteroid, in 1801. He called it Ceres. It is the largest known asteroid, 932km across – big enough for Piazzi to spot it with his fairly simple telescope. Asteroids reflect the Sun's light, making them shine and sparkle – 'asteroid' means 'small star-like object'.

▼ Most asteroids are smaller than houses, but a few are bigger than Earth's largest mountains.

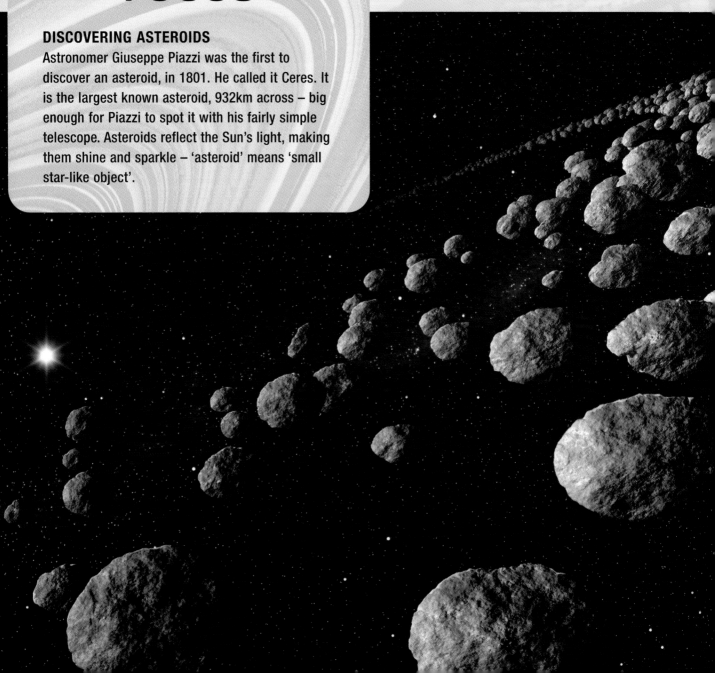

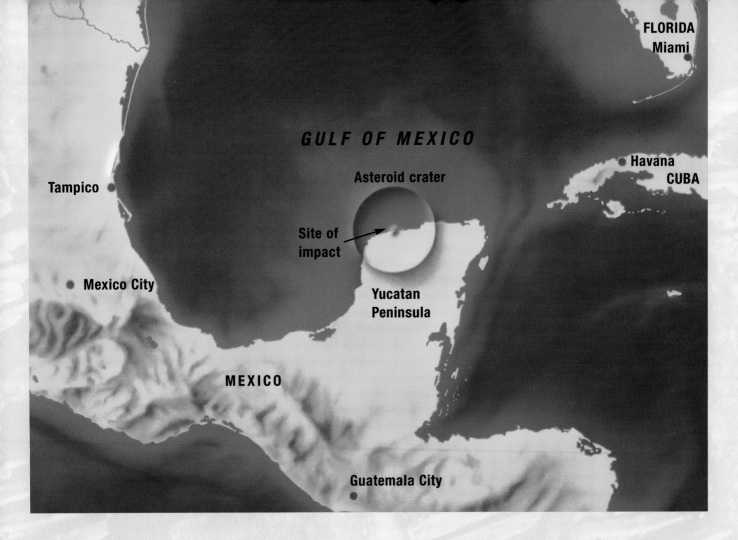

The map shows the Gulf of Mexico region including Tampico, Mexico City, Mexico, Yucatan Peninsula, Guatemala City, Havana, Cuba, Florida and Miami, with the Asteroid crater and Site of impact marked.

FLORIDA
Miami

GULF OF MEXICO

Havana
CUBA

Asteroid crater

Tampico

Site of impact

Mexico City

Yucatan
Peninsula

MEXICO

Guatemala City

THE ASTEROID BELT

More than nine-tenths of all asteroids go around the Sun in a huge, flat ring called the Asteroid Belt. This is between Mars and Jupiter, separating the inner planets from the outer gas giants. The belt is about 200 million kilometres wide. On average, its larger asteroids are six million kilometres apart. They spin and tumble as they orbit the Sun.

TYPES AND SIZES

There are millions of asteroids, ranging in size from a few metres to many kilometres across. But only a few are really big, from 200 to 1,000 kilometres. These are sometimes called 'minor planets'. Every now and then asteroids smash into each other and break into pieces, making smaller objects which are called meteoroids.

Asteroids can be divided into three main types, depending on what they contain. Carbonaceous asteroids are mostly made up of carbon-rich rock, similar to coal, and

▲ About 65 million years ago an asteroid 10km wide may have smashed into Earth on the coast of Mexico. It is thought to have caused a massive 200km crater, which is now partly hidden under seabed mud.

usually have a dark colour. Silicaceous asteroids are brighter and contain both rock and metal. Metallic asteroids are mostly made up of the metals iron and nickel.

OTHER ASTEROIDS

Some asteroids are not in the Asteroid Belt. They follow their own lonely orbits, mainly among the inner planets. There are also two groups of asteroids, called the Trojans, which follow the same orbit as Jupiter. One group is in front of the planet, the other is behind.

DESTINATION EARTH?

A few asteroids have orbits that bring them close to Earth. Very rarely one crashes into our planet and leaves a large bowl-like crater. Telescopes and satellites watch the skies carefully in case, one day, an asteroid is detected heading our way.

COMETS AND METEOROIDS

Comets and meteoroids are small objects, mainly made of rock, dust or ice, that fly around the Solar System. Some of them come close enough to Earth to be seen in the sky – or even smash into the ground.

THE OORT CLOUD

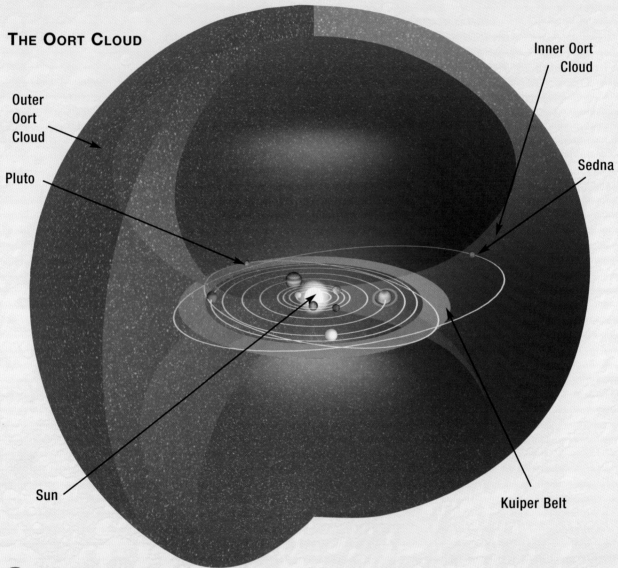

Inner Oort Cloud

Outer Oort Cloud

Sedna

Pluto

Sun

Kuiper Belt

COMET CLOUD

Comets are lumps of 'dirty ice' – rock, dust, snow and ice – orbiting the Sun. They are usually a few kilometres across. The Solar System is surrounded by a huge, ball-shaped cloud of billions of comets, known as the Oort Cloud. This

▲ The planets mostly orbit the Sun in a flat disc shape. But the Oort Cloud is ball-shaped and its comets orbit the Sun at all angles.

reaches as far as 14,000 billion kilometres from the Sun – many times farther than the orbit of Pluto.

COMETS IN CLOSE-UP

Sometimes a comet's orbit brings it out of the Oort Cloud and closer to the Sun. When this happens, the 'dirty ice' turns to gases and forms a large, glowing 'head' around the comet, called a coma. Gases and dust form two 'tails'. The gas tail is faint and blue, and the dust tail is white and bright. If a comet flies near to Earth on its orbit, we can see it even without a telescope. Some comets come near every few years, others visit our region much more rarely.

METEOROIDS

Meteoroids are small bits of space rock or metal that have fallen off comets or asteroids. Comets leave a stream of meteoroids behind them as they zoom along. Meteoroids also form when asteroids collide and break up. Meteoroids are found moving in all directions all around the Solar System.

METEORS AND METEORITES

If a meteoroid comes too close to a planet, gravity pulls it in. A meteor is a meteoroid that has been pulled by Earth's gravity. As it falls into the atmosphere and rubs against the air, it heats up and burns with a bright streak of light. This shows up in the dark sky as a 'shooting star'.

▲ Halley's Comet passes Earth every 76 years. This photograph, taken on its last visit in 1986, shows its brighter dust tail and fainter, longer gas tail.

completely, it falls all the way to Earth's surface and is called a meteorite. About 3,000 meteorites hit Earth every year.

WATCHING THE SKIES

For thousands of years, people have looked at the sky by day and night, and tried to understand the Sun, Moon, stars and planets. Often their ideas were mixed up with religion, myths and magic.

FIRST IDEAS

As long as 30,000 years ago, early people saw patterns in the stars, which we now call the constellations. Most of them believed that Earth stayed still in the centre of everything, while the objects far above moved around it.

Many also believed that the Sun, Moon and stars represented powerful gods and spirits.

From about 6,000 years ago, some ancient people used the regular movements of the Sun, Moon, planets and stars to measure the

► Nicolaus Copernicus suggested that the Sun was at the centre of the Solar System, and also realised that objects like the Sun and Moon seem to go around Earth because the Earth itself spins.

passing of time. They made the first calendars. Ptolemy of ancient Greece was one of the first great astronomers – experts in watching the skies and studying stars and other objects in space.

PLANETS

Mercury, Mars, Venus, Jupiter and Saturn are the only planets we can see with our own eyes, rather than through telescopes. So these were the only planets that ancient people could study. But long ago, the differences between the stars and planets were not clear. Even the Sun and Moon were sometimes called 'planets'.

SEEING THE TRUTH

More than 2,000 years ago in ancient Greece, Aristarchus of Samos suggested that planets went around the Sun rather than Earth. No one took much notice. In the sixteenth century Nicolaus Copernicus had the same idea. He worked out that the movements of the Sun, Moon and planets only made sense if the Sun was in the middle.

SOLAR SYSTEM SIGHTS

As well as five Solar System planets, the Moon, comets and shooting stars are all visible without a telescope. Astronomy magazines, books and websites have information about where and when to look for them. Some of the most exciting events are eclipses. A lunar eclipse happens when the Earth comes between the Sun and the Moon. Earth's shadow falls across the Moon, making it darker. A solar eclipse happens when the Moon passes between Earth and the Sun. The Moon blocks out the Sun for a short time – and part of the world goes dark.

◄ Stonehenge in southern England was built over 4,000 years ago, probably as an observatory and calendar. On Midsummer's Day the rising Sun shines through the middle of the pattern of huge stones.

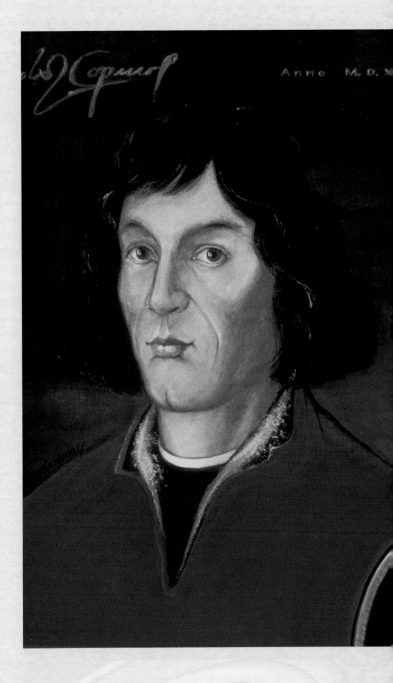

EVIDENCE FOCUS

HOW TO WATCH A SOLAR ECLIPSE

Because looking at the Sun is so dangerous, solar eclipses must be viewed indirectly, as follows. Make a tiny hole in the middle of a sheet of white card, by carefully pushing a pin through it. Hold this up so the Sun shines through it. Hold another piece of white card about 30cm below and angle it so that a small image of the Sun appears on it. When the Moon starts to move in front of the Sun, you can watch it on the lower card.

TELESCOPES

A telescope makes faraway objects look nearer and bigger, so it is easier to see them in detail. The invention of the telescope had an enormous effect on the study of space and the Solar System.

THE FIRST TELESCOPES

The telescope was probably invented by a Dutch lens-maker, Hans Lippershey, in about 1608. People already knew that lenses (curved pieces of glass) could magnify things – make them look bigger. Lippershey positioned two lenses in a tube, to make the magnification far greater. His invention was

▼ Galileo's new telescope allowed him to discover very faint stars, mountains on the Moon, and also moons going around Jupiter. But his colleagues were interested in its use for spying on enemies in wartime.

intended for spying on the enemy during wartime. But in 1609 in Italy, scientist Galileo Galilei realised a telescope would be perfect for looking into space. He built his own version and quickly began studying the skies.

MORE TYPES OF TELESCOPES

Telescopes that work using light rays are called optical telescopes. But there are other kinds too. Radio telescopes detect invisible radio waves given out by objects in space. These telescopes look like huge television satellite dishes or radio aerials. They show us distant galaxies, exploding stars and echoes from the Big Bang. Infrared telescopes detect heat or infrared rays, and X-ray telescopes sense X-rays. All these waves come naturally from various objects in space.

EVIDENCE FOCUS

IMPROVE YOUR VIEW!
Astronomy shops, science stores and some camera shops sell small reflector and refractor telescopes for looking at the night sky. A telescope's power is measured by the size of its main mirror or lens. A 75mm refractor or a 100mm reflector makes a good starter telescope. Alternatively, a pair of binoculars is like two small refractor telescopes fixed together. 10 x 50 binoculars make objects look 10 times bigger and have 50mm lenses.

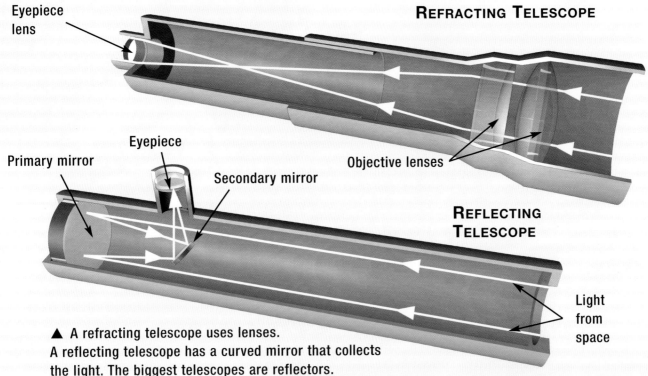

Eyepiece lens

Primary mirror

Eyepiece

Secondary mirror

Objective lenses

REFLECTING TELESCOPE

Light from space

▲ A refracting telescope uses lenses. A reflecting telescope has a curved mirror that collects the light. The biggest telescopes are reflectors.

OBSERVATORIES

An observatory is a place – usually a building – where astronomers watch the skies. Most observatories have a dome-shaped roof which can be opened for telescopes to point out at the sky. Observatories are often built on mountain-tops in remote areas, away from bright city lights and pollution such as smog. Radio observatories have dish-like radio telescopes.

WATCHING FROM SPACE

Telescopes on Earth's surface have to look through Earth's atmosphere into space. This blurs their view, and clouds and bad weather get in the way. So some telescopes are now sent by rockets into orbit around Earth. In space, they have a much clearer view.

▶ The Hubble Space Telescope, launched in 1990, goes around Earth once every 97 minutes at an average height of 600km.

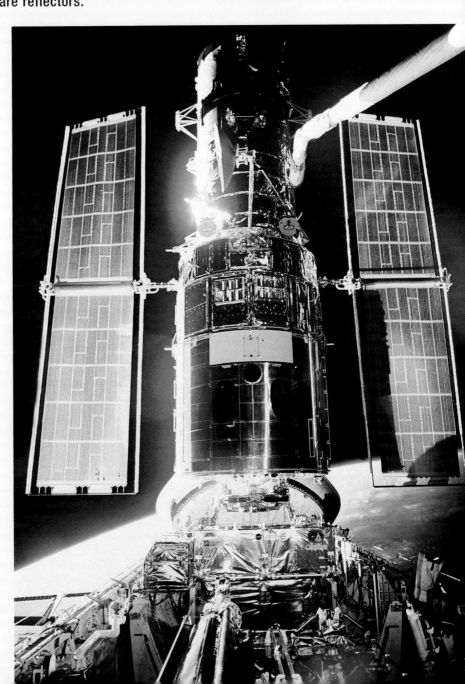

SPACE EXPLORATION

During centuries of staring up at the Solar System, people longed to leave Earth and explore it themselves. But this has only happened in the past 50 years. Space exploration is still just beginning.

ROCKET SCIENCE

The only engine powerful enough to go into space is a rocket engine. Simple powder-fuel, firework-style rockets were invented in ancient China over a thousand years ago. In the 1920s, scientists began building bigger rocket engines using liquid fuels. During the Second World War (1939–1945) these were used as missile weapons to carry bombs. Then after the war, scientists began working on space rockets. In 1957, Russian scientists made a rocket powerful enough to carry the first artificial object into space, to orbit the Earth. This was the satellite Sputnik 1.

LIVE CARGO

Sputnik 1 was small, simple and successful. But no one knew if living things could travel in space. Soon after Sputnik 1, the bigger craft Sputnik 2 carried a dog named Laika into orbit. She survived for a time and proved that life could continue in a spacecraft. Sadly, there was no way to bring her back to Earth.

In 1961, Russian cosmonaut (astronaut) Yuri Gagarin became the first person in space. He made one orbit in his spacecraft, Vostok 1, and returned safely. Soon American astronauts followed. Today, hundreds of people have been

▶ Sputnik 1 was a hollow metal ball about 60cm across with four long antennae (aerials). It sent radio signals back to Earth for 21 days.

▶ The US Space Shuttle can carry a crew of up to ten people. It is launched by its own three rocket engines and two rocket boosters, and carries its fuel in a massive dark tank. It glides back to Earth to be used again.

into space, and hundreds of satellites are in Earth orbit. Different kinds of satellites take pictures of Earth and space, measure rays of various kinds, monitor the weather, and beam radio, television, telephone and Internet signals all around the world.

LIFE ON OTHER PLANETS

Writers and film-makers have dreamed up all kinds of alien life forms. But there is little evidence that they exist. The other planets in the Solar System could not support the type of life we have on Earth. Our kind of life needs liquid water. Other planets and moons either do not have water, or they are so hot or cold that water cannot exist as a liquid.

Some experts think that life may have existed on Mars millions of years ago, when it had liquid water. Also there could be different kinds of life that we do not yet understand. And there could also be life beyond the Solar System. For now, we do not know – but we can have fun imagining.

FACT FOCUS

LIFE ON MARS?

In 1996, scientists studied a meteorite which seemed to contain preserved remains, or fossils, of microscopic worm-like creatures. The meteorite probably came originally from Mars, where it was knocked into space by another meteorite, and landed on Earth 13,000 years ago. The 'fossils' could show that simple life once existed on Mars, but scientists disagree about them.

SPACE PROBES

Many fantastic pictures of the Sun, planets and moons have been taken by space probes. These are remote-controlled spacecraft, without people, that can travel to the edge of the Solar System – and beyond.

PROBE MISSIONS

A space probe explores a certain region of space and sends back images and other information, like measurements of temperature, X-rays and other rays. All this information comes back as radio signals. Most probes are programmed for a particular task or mission. Many are part-automatic, with on-board navigation systems to help them find their way. But they can also be controlled and adjusted by radio signals from Earth.

Because space probes have no crew, they do not have to carry complicated life-support equipment or return safely to Earth. They can travel huge distances across the Solar System, on journeys lasting many years.

FAMOUS PROBES

The first space probe, Luna 1, was sent to the Moon in 1959. Since then, probes have visited planets, the Sun, asteroids and comets. The probe Galileo, named after the great astronomer, was launched in 1989. It went to Jupiter and took amazing photos of the planet and its moons. In 2003, at the end of its working life, it was deliberately crashed into Jupiter's swirling gases.

PROBE LANDERS

As well as fly-past probes, there are lander probes. These touch down on other planets or moons to study their gases and rocks. The Mars Pathfinder probe was launched in 1996 and landed on Mars in 1997. It carried a small six-wheeled robot vehicle or rover, Sojourner, to explore the surface. In 2004 the Mars Exploration Rover mission landed two bigger rovers, Spirit and Opportunity, on the 'Red Planet'.

The Saturn probe Cassini, launched in 1997, carried a lander named Huygens. This parachuted down to the surface of Saturn's largest moon, Titan, in 2005. Huygens took pictures of Titan's landscape and tested the surface for various chemicals. It found that Titan has lakes and rain made of liquid methane.

◄ Sojourner was the first vehicle ever to travel on the surface of another planet. This view from its lander shows the tea-tray-sized rover near a large Martian rock called Yogi.

▲ This artist's picture shows Voyager 2 on its six-hour fly-past of the gas giant Uranus in 1986.

The probes that have travelled farthest are Voyager 1 and Voyager 2. They were launched in 1977 to study the gas giant outer planets and their moons. Voyager 2 managed to fly past four planets, since they were all in the correct positions during its mission for a 'Grand Tour'. Both Voyagers have now gone beyond the orbit of the farthest planet, Pluto, and left the main Solar System.

A MESSAGE FOR ALIENS
Voyagers 1 and 2 are still heading away from the Solar System, to the depths of space. Voyager 1 is now more than 10,000 million kilometres away. Both of these probes carry information or data plates, including recordings of greetings in 55 different languages and Earth sounds such as whale song and pop music.

▶ Both the Voyager and Galileo probes have photographed Jupiter's moon Io. Volcanic eruptions are common at its surface – here at the upper left and top centre.

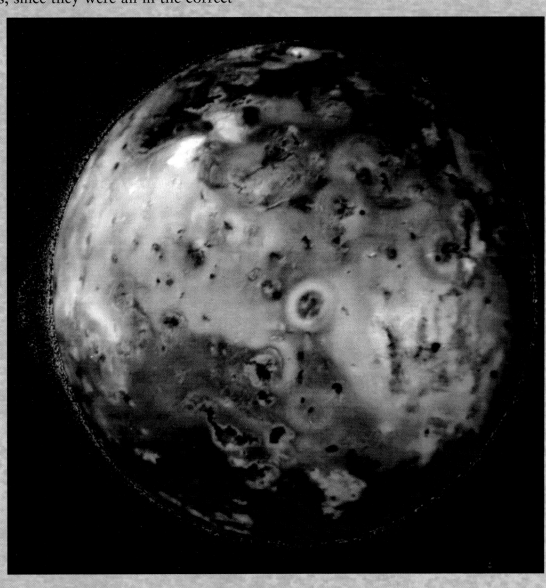

VISITING THE SOLAR SYSTEM

The Solar System is tiny compared to the rest of space. But the distances between the planets are big enough to make interplanetary travel for people very difficult indeed.

WALKING ON THE MOON

The only Solar System object that people have visited so far is the Moon. During the 1960s the USA planned the Apollo series of missions. The early three-person Apollo craft orbited Earth. Apollos 8 and 10 orbited the Moon. Then in July 1969, Apollo 11 made the first Moon landing. Astronauts Neil Armstrong and

▲ Buzz Aldrin on the Moon with the Apollo 11 landing craft, the Lunar Module (left). With no rain or wind, his boot prints in the dust are still there.

Edwin 'Buzz' Aldrin were the first humans to walk on its surface, while third crew member Michael Collins stayed in the Moon orbiter. The whole mission took eight days.

◄ The International Space Station (ISS) is visited regularly by robot craft bringing supplies. It also receives craft ferrying up new crew members to replace the returning ones.

STAYING ALIVE

Space probes can travel huge distances over many years. However, spacecraft with people on board are much more limited. The craft must carry enough food, oxygen and other supplies for the journey. It should be big enough for the crew to live in, and be designed to return safely to Earth. Also it is hard for the crew to spend so long trapped in a tiny spacecraft, far from Earth, with no gravity or way of escape. This is why, so far, no one has made a space journey to another planet.

SPACE STATIONS

After Apollo 11, five more Apollo missions made Moon landings, until 1972. Then long-distance space travel was put aside in favour of space stations in orbit around Earth. A space station is a long-term base where astronauts can stay and work. The long-lived Russian Mir Space Station lasted from 1986 to 2001. The much larger ISS (International Space Station) received its first crew in 2000.

GOING FARTHER

Experts have started to plan more trips to the Moon, and perhaps even to the planet Mars. The Mars trip would be more than 100 million kilometres – one hundred times farther than a Moon mission. The astronauts would have to stay on Mars for several months, waiting for Earth and Mars to line up in the best way for them to return. So the whole mission there and back could last up to two years.

FACT FOCUS

YOUR WEIGHT ON OTHER PLANETS

A planet's gravity depends not on its size but on its mass – the amount of substance or matter in it. The stronger its gravity, the harder it pulls on objects, and so the more the objects weigh. This chart shows what a 50kg person would weigh on the Solar System's nine planets plus our Moon.

Planet	Weight	Planet	Weight
Mercury	19 kg	Jupiter	120 kg
Venus	45 kg	Saturn	46 kg
Earth	50 kg	Uranus	44 kg
Moon	8 kg	Neptune	56 kg
Mars	19 kg	Pluto	3 kg

TIMELINE

Here are some of the main discoveries and milestones in the history of space science, and our studies and exploration of the Solar System and beyond.

30,000–10,000 BC
Early people depict what look like constellations in rock art and ivory carvings.

ABOUT 3000 BC
The ancient Egyptians use the positions of the stars to make calendars to help with the farming seasons.

3000–2000 BC
Stonehenge is built in England, possibly as a kind of calendar to mark the changing position of the Sun.

2500 BC–AD 100
Ancient Greek and Chinese scholars study astronomy and note the movements of the planets.

250 BC
Greek scholar Aristarchus of Samos (310–230 BC) is the first to realise that Earth moves around the Sun, but other Greek astronomers ignore his ideas.

AD 150
Greek scientist Ptolemy (AD 85–165) proposes his theory that the Sun, Moon and planets all revolve around Earth. This idea, though not correct, dominates astronomy for the next 1,500 years.

AD 500
The Mayans of Central America study the skies, make calendars and build observatories for watching the sky at night.

AD 900
Arabic scholars in the Middle East build on Ptolemy's work, studying the planets and making star charts. The science of astronomy flourishes in Baghdad, in what is now Iraq.

1054
Arabic, Chinese, Japanese and Native American astronomers record a star burning amazingly brightly for several weeks. It was a supernova, now called the Taurus supernova.

1543
At the end of his life, Polish astronomer Nicolaus Copernicus (1473–1543) publishes a book about his belief that the Sun must be in the middle of the Solar System, with Earth and the other planets orbiting around it.

1572
Danish astronomer Tycho Brahe (1546–1601) observes a supernova. He later studies comets, builds an observatory and writes many books about astronomy.

1604
German astronomer and mathematician Johannes Kepler (1571–1630) observes a new star, later called Kepler's star.

1608
Dutch lens-maker Hans Lippershey invents the refracting telescope, the first type of telescope.

1609
Italian astronomer Galileo Galilei (1564–1642) makes his own telescope and uses it to study the Solar System. He claims, like Copernicus, that Earth moves around the Sun. Religious leaders try to suppress his work.

1668
English scientist Isaac Newton (1643–1727) builds the first working reflecting telescope.

1781
German-born British astronomer William Herschel (1738–1822) discovers Uranus, the first new planet to be identified since ancient times.

1801
Italian astronomer Giuseppe Piazzi (1746–1826) discovers Ceres, the first known and largest asteroid.

1846
German astronomer Johann Galle (1812–1910) discovers the planet Neptune, after other astronomers predict that another planet must exist, because the movement of Uranus indicates another planet beyond pulling on it.

1877
Italian astronomer Giovanni Schiaparelli (1835–1910) observes what he calls 'channels' on Mars. But this term is translated as 'canals', suggesting someone dug them, which started a debate about whether life might exist on Mars.

1927
Belgian physicist George Lemaître (1894–1966) suggests that the Universe began with a huge explosion, which later is known as the Big Bang.

1930
US astronomer Clyde Tombaugh (1906–1997) discovers the planet Pluto.

1937
US astronomer and engineer Grote Reber (1911–2002) designs and builds the first radio telescope.

1957
In October, Sputnik 1 is the first artificial satellite to go into orbit around Earth. It is followed in November by Sputnik 2 carrying a dog, Laika.

1958
The USA government's space agency, NASA (National Aeronautics and Space Administration) is set up to run American space exploration.

1959
The USSR sends the first ever space probe, Luna 1, which flies close to the Moon. It is the first artificial object to leave Earth's gravity.

1961
Russian jet pilot Yuri Gagarin (1934–1968) goes into Earth orbit aboard Vostok 1, becoming the first person in space.

1963
Russian pilot-parachutist Valentina Tereshkova (born 1937) becomes the first woman in space, spending three days in orbit around Earth aboard Vostok 6.

1969
The USA's Apollo 11 mission reaches the Moon, and US astronauts Neil Armstrong (born 1930) and Buzz Aldrin (born 1930) land in the Lunar Module to explore its surface.

1971
The first space station is launched by the USSR (now Russia and CIS), named Salyut 1.

1977
The USA launches the space probes Voyager 1 and 2 to study the outer planets. They are still travelling through space, far from the main Solar System.

1981
The USA launches the first Space Shuttle, a reusable plane-shaped spacecraft.

1990
The Hubble Space Telescope is sent into orbit around Earth to observe and capture images of space and objects in it.

1996
Space scientists studying a meteorite thought to come from Mars discover a microscopic fossil-like shape, which could indicate that life once existed there.

1997
The USA's Pathfinder space probe lands on Mars. Its robot explorer, Sojourner, becomes the first vehicle to travel on another planet.

2003
US astronomers discover a tenth planet-like object orbiting the Sun and name it 2003 VB12. It is later renamed Sedna and some experts claim it is a tenth planet, though others disagree.

2005
The Huygens lander, launched from the Cassini-Huygens probe, lands on Saturn's moon Titan. It is the first artificial object to land on another planet's moon, and the first to touch down on an object in the outer Solar System.

2005
Astronomers announce another 'tenth planet', an object named 2003 UB313. Arguments continue over whether Sedna, UB313 and even Pluto are true planets.

GLOSSARY

asteroid A lump of rock and/or metal, smaller than a planet and most moons, which orbits the Sun.

Asteroid Belt The region where most asteroids orbit the Sun, between Mars and Jupiter.

astronomy The study of stars, planets, moons and other objects in space.

atmosphere A layer of gases surrounding a planet or star.

axis An imaginary line passing through the middle of a star or planet, around which it spins or rotates.

Big Bang A huge explosion, thought to have happened at the beginning of the Universe.

black hole A very dark, squashed area of space with very powerful gravity, created when a huge star collapses.

coma A bright cloud around a comet.

comet A small ball of rock and ice on a long orbit around the Sun.

constellation A pattern or picture that people imagine in the stars as they are viewed from here on Earth.

core The central part of a planet, moon, star or other space object.

corona The faint glowing layer of gases surrounding the Sun.

crater A dish-shaped hollow on a planet, moon or asteroid, caused by another object crashing into it.

crust The rocky outer layer of a planet such as Earth.

day The amount of time it takes a planet or moon to spin around once.

dwarf star A star smaller than the Sun.

eclipse When one space object, such as a moon, goes between another and the Sun and casts a shadow.

equator An imaginary line around the middle of a space object such as a planet or moon.

galaxy A huge group of millions of stars, planets and other objects in space, held together by gravity.

giant star A star that is considerably bigger than the Sun.

gravity A pulling force possessed by any matter (material or substance). Stars have so much matter, their gravity is very strong.

Kuiper Belt A ring of comets and comet-like objects in the outer Solar System, beyond Neptune.

lander A spacecraft, or part of one, designed to land on a space object like a planet, moon or asteroid.

lens A curved piece of glass or clear plastic that bends light.

lunar To do with Earth's moon, called the Moon.

lunar eclipse When Earth passes between the Sun and the Moon, casting a shadow on the Moon.

mantle A layer of rock or other materials that lies between the core and the outer layers of a planet or moon.

mass Matter or substance, usually made of tiny particles called atoms.

meteor A meteoroid that enters the Earth's atmosphere and burns up, appearing as a bright streak of light.

meteorite A meteor that falls to the Earth's surface.

meteoroid A small chunk which has broken from a comet or asteroid.

moon A space object that orbits a planet. The moon of planet Earth is called the Moon, with a capital 'M'.

nebula A cloud of gas and dust in space, which may be millions of times bigger than a star, or thrown off by a dying star (planetary nebula).

observatory A building or place where telescopes are used to observe (study) space.

Oort Cloud A huge, ball-shaped cloud of comets surrounding the Solar System.

orbit To go around another object. The orbit of a Solar System planet like the Earth is its path around the Sun.

planet A large object orbiting a star.

radar A way of measuring shapes and distances by bouncing radio waves off a surface and detecting the reflections or echoes.

satellite Any object that orbits another object in space. Natural satellites include planets around the Sun and moons around a planet. Artificial satellites include space stations and what we simply call 'satellites' around Earth.

shooting star Another name for a meteor.

solar To do with the Sun.

solar eclipse When the Moon passes between the Sun and Earth, blocking out the Sun's light as seen from Earth.

Solar System The Sun and all the planets and other objects that orbit it, plus their own moons and similar objects.

space probe A small spacecraft with no crew, sent to explore space and send information back to Earth.

space station A space base orbiting Earth where astronauts can stay and work for long periods.

sunspot A dark area on the Sun's surface.

supergiant star The biggest and brightest type of star.

supernova The explosion at the end of a supergiant star's life.

telescope A device that makes faraway things look bigger.

Universe Everything that exists everywhere in all of space.

year The amount of time it takes a planet to complete one orbit around a star.

FURTHER INFORMATION

Books to read

DK Space Encyclopedia by Heather Couper and Nigel Henbest (Dorling Kindersley, 1999)

Earthling's Guide to Deep Space: Explore the Galaxy Through the Eye of the Hubble Space Telescope by Carolyn Sumners and Kerry Handron (McGraw-Hill Education, 1999)

Explore Space by Ian Graham (Dorling Kindersley, 2004)

Horrible Science: Space, Stars and Slimy Aliens by Nick Arnold and Tony De Saulles (Scholastic Hippo, 2004)

The Moon Landing by Paul Mason (Hodder Wayland, 2002)

Space Dramas by Chris Woodford (Belitha Press, 2002)

Space Travel by Stuart Atkinson (Belitha Press, 2002)

The Usborne Internet-Linked Complete Book of Astronomy and Space by Alistair Smith (Usborne Publishing, 2001)

Websites

NASA for Kids
http://www.nasa.gov/audience/forkids/home/index.html
Kids' site run by NASA, the space agency of the USA, with vast amounts of information about space and space travel.

Views of the Solar System
http://www.solarviews.com/eng/homepage.htm
Hundreds of beautiful pictures and animations of the Solar System's planets, moons and other features.

INDEX